The Blainville Testament

Narrative Poems

Sydney Lea

Down East Books
Camden, Maine

For my brother Jake

Down East Books

An imprint of The Globe Pequot Publishing Group, Inc.
64 South Main Street
Essex, Connecticut 06426
www.globepequot.com

Copyright © 1992 by Sydney Lea
First Down East edition published in 2026
Originally published in 1992 by Story Line Press. Reprinted by permission.

All rights reserved. No part of this book may be reproduced in any form or by any electronic or mechanical means, including information storage and retrieval systems, without written permission from the publisher, except by a reviewer who may quote passages in a review.

British Library Cataloguing in Publication Information available

Library of Congress Cataloging-in-Publication Data available
ISBN 9781684752331 (paperback) | ISBN 9781684752850 (epub)

CONTENTS

Proem : After George's Axe Was Stolen 5

I. THE BLAINVILLE TESTAMENT
    The Blainville Testament 11

II. AT THE EDGE
    Riverfront 27
    Upcountry Speedway 29
    In the Alley 31
    Spite: Her Tale 34
    At the Edge 41
    Road Agent 43
    Revision: Early December 47
    Insomnia: The Distances 49
    The Hitch-hiker 53
    Private Boys' School, 3rd Grade 57
    Black Bear Cuffing for Food 59
    Wyoming 61
    In the Blind 63
    Wedding Anniversary 66

III. THE FEUD
    The Feud 71

IV. MANLEY
    Manley 91

PROEM: AFTER GEORGE'S AXE WAS STOLEN

I came back to camp at nightfall,
a scene that, wanting an object, had changed:
How old my dooryard pine had grown,
the woodpeckers having their way.
Above my lumber pile,
decay in a shimmer rose.

I said aloud, "I ought to do something."

I heard the hidden owls' redundancies,
but where was the nighthawk,
his solid bang of wing
as he fell like a heavy blade through a haze of mayflies?
Where were the mayflies?
Wood lice were turning my cabin's timbers to lace.

It was his, but he left it to me.

Far off, the last of the logging trains.
I shouldn't merely hug myself, I thought,
rocking back and forth
on this granite slab that the river slaps
and ceaselessly slaps
until one day it breaks through.

I ought to go someplace.

On this long shelf where water
expends itself as froth in the Giant Eddy
—where so often we sat while George sang
or told from his monumental store of stories
that made of life a shape:
all that motion, action!—

I sat down and wept.

Once I had saved the axe's handle
from porcupines who fretted it for salt
and didn't care to whom it belonged.
The head had such authority:
six pounds and a half of metal, forged to endure,
whatever the incidental

sallies of rust, of rain gone acid.

He'd brag on the heaps of railroad ties he could pile
in a single day,
out with axe and lantern before the dawn,
back after dark the same way,
for a whole long season
never to see his shack but under stars.

Like this one.

Air passed without resistance
through the kitchen corner
where the axe had stood for years,
used only so that my children might see
how it cleaved the staunchest stovewood
as if it were foam.

Maybe that was it. Children.

Who else would break in and take
no other thing that the world might value?
Unless it were someone else who loved him...
unless it were someone
who also sits just now,
things before his eyes transformed, dispersed,

as a far locomotive faintly cries,

and a boulder moon on the rise
behind a fragile shack and a gnarled pine
scatters these little star-like shapes
on ledge till it looks like a sieve—
wondering, "Where shall I go?"
wondering, "What shall I do?"

THE BLAINVILLE TESTAMENT

THE BLAINVILLE TESTAMENT
—*for Mark Jarman and Robert McDowell*

I remember how that canny man Montaigne
wrote that all philosophy consists
in learning how to die. Not that to tell
this tale will be my death. But I want it right.
Nor that philosophy is what I'm after;
words, rather—the way that strung together

they help things last. Or may. I put them here
because of late the spoken ones come hard,
for want of conversation and of breath.
It's how they can both take and give back shape
I love. For much that we call love attaches
to eloquence in things, if you can catch it:

Creases in a favorite pair of shoes.
A certain slant of light, as the White Nun said,
on winter afternoons. Or odors, timbres,
sounds. Whatever craves and begs translation.
Think of a favorite cup whose dents and scratches,
if you could merely find their proper order,

make runic narrative of all your mornings.
Your chimney's sibilants, whiffs of a bush.
Feel of your hand along a porch's rail.
I have a special stake in this, you see.
You'll see, that is, if I can rightly show
the things that I've attended all these years,

and more important, what they've said to me
in spite of all my neighbors' bleak assurance
that I would never comprehend this country.
"A lawyer!" so they huffed, "and from the city!"
I'm sick to death with all of that, as well
as with The Crab. And yet, although he prods,

he is a friend. Or maybe he's a she,
as the late insurance man (a lawyer, too)
lately put it: "Death is the mother of beauty,
within whose burning bosom we devise
our earthly mothers waiting, sleeplessly."
Oh, I have memorized the fine devices!

Lord knows my poor old-womanish bosom burns
and I'm sleepless here, mothering The Crab,
The Crab my mother. We get on together,
especially with the moon out there so brilliant.
We see across the meadows to The Bald Man,
and summon other forms as well — the spruces

I once knew, the barred owls crouching in them.
Hardwoods too, their shadows on the snow,
there! and there! and there and there and there!
In mind, I travel through them, breathing cool,
as I did one winter to visit Billy Fields,
six months after Blainville cut him dead,

except as a kind of allegoric figure,
referred to for the sake of local color.
If you're from here, you'll know just what I mean,
and what it's meant to me, his confidant.
But if you're not, you'll want me to explain.
And I'll oblige, since I am in no hurry,

and since I'm not yet sure whom I write *for*.
It may be I address myself alone.
Should you take interest, though, then you must hear
—as I, arrived post facto, heard—of Mark.
Town legend calls him Billy's Victim still,
a designation I'll leave you to judge.

This boy was smart, which word here signifies
something like handy, or quick to learn, or both.
He was among our first to drive a car,
the first to plumb or rig a house with light.
Others could hit a ball from plate to pond
as he could do, but only Mark would have

some slick machine downcellar to make his bat!
He didn't drink. He didn't chew or curse,
and loved—a thing for local praise—to work.
Shiftless Brian Hart would ask him up
to his hunting camp on The Bald Man and pray for sleet,
so Mark, all cabin-feverish, would tend

whatever needed fixing on Hart's shack.
"Last fall was good," joked Brian once. "It hailed.
The roof leaked through until he patched it up
with half a shingle and seven common nails!"
Mark grinned and kicked his boot-toe in the dust.
Hart's trick had been no trick. Mark wasn't fooled,

just, as always, happy to oblige.
A paragon, in brief, in every sense—
moving-picture handsome, a hero's posture,
teeth that might be wrought from dearest marble,
an automatic decency. He was
model and darling both. He had a way

of knowing what to do to help a neighbor
before the neighbor knew. Especially elders.
Elsie Cammon's cow once choked to death
on a backwoods apple. (Her fence was never much,
became a local trope: a man might say
"tight as Elsie's fence," if he meant loose.

Though all was change then, still the region spoke
a language brightly eloquent of place,
of men and women working in the place,
though it was often mean, like "kind as Fields,"
or "Elsie's face is rough as a bag of hammers,"
or—as I've heard—"windy as city lawyers...._")

Billy went that day with Mark to see
the cow put underground. No one knows why.
I whose lawyer's job it was to sort
Mark's tiny leavings—I can say at least
the darkest rumor is a fantasy:
"murder for money?" There wasn't any money!

Whatever for, old Fields went out with Mark.
Mark had used a kind of home-made tractor
to drag the cow back further in the woods.
He'd ploughed a hole, and meant to roll her in.
How Billy cursed and grumbled at such waste
in telling me! But be that as it may,

Mark was set to heave the poor beast in
when he dropped his brand-new watch in the brand-new grave.
(He'd had it in his shirt, according to Billy,
which struck the town as odd, to say it mildly.)
Mark jumped down to fetch it, the ground gave way,
and half a ton of beef fell in upon him.

A radical story some here still expound
was that Billy shoved the cow. "At 79?"
So I would ask. "He moved eight hundred pounds?"
"Never mind. He shoved her with the tractor."
(That he'd never seen a motor didn't matter.)
The commoner accusation, less extreme,

was that Billy sat and watched Mark bleed to death
from wounds the rib-bones made along his side.
The service that at last can fall to me
is letting Billy tell us his own version.
No one, while he lived, would ever ask it
face to face of him. And *I 've* suppressed it

all these years. "A lawyer's sworn to silence,"
so I'd claim (my little irony).
For nothing I could say would make a difference.
The town already felt it was suspicious
that I was Billy's counsel at the hearing
and also settled Mark's so-called estate.

Of course who else would do such chores back then?
But there was talk. And let them go on talking
when —like all my characters— I'm gone.
I cannot care. For better or for worse,
they'll know me now, and so will you, whoever
you may be. This last account's for me.

It is! I write to hear the voice of Billy,
to watch the landscape quicken as I listen.
    "Make no mistake, Judge...." (Billy called me Judge
right from the start, and wouldn't be corrected.)
    "Judge, I'll tell you, never mind the gossip.
I liked that boy, and that boy liked me too,

"as good as anyone, though I'm a man
who should have died before he drew a breath.
That's what they'll tell you now that Mark is dead.
It took his death to make me out a Devil;
they didn't talk that way before he died.
I did what I could do. I meant to save him.

"But you know what we had back then for traffic.
I had to go on foot, and it was hot,
and it was all uphill, a mile at least,
from way out there until I reached the flat,
and almost that again down to the tar.
If you could see me sweat! And my old heart,

"like a bagged hen! I wanted him to live,
but did his life mean Billy had to die?
I asked myself. They'd call that selfish, Judge,
but could they say what good it would have done
for both of us to go? Oh yes, I've heard:
'If Blainville had to up and lose the one,

"too bad it couldn't get shut of the other.'
As if the things that drove this town to hell
were all my doing. As if I was a wizard.
If I had died, would that young man come back?
Well, they believe it somehow. Never mind.
I had to stop for breath, and that was that.

"I lay against that twisty pasture pine
in Simpsons' field. (That tree is lively yet.
You wonder how many birds have rigged a nest
in all its boughs, how many spots of dew
and rain and snow have come to it and gone,
how many bugs have hidden in its bark.

"You wonder at those things. At least I do....)
I lay against the trunk and, looking up,
saw one of those big buzzards looking down.
We had them in those days, but they were rare,
so maybe I was dozing even then.
'I hope he'll let me die before he comes.'

"I said those words out loud, I think, as if
to say a thing out loud could make a spell.
I didn't want to die at all, you see.
I'd go in comfort anyway, I thought.
The sun was out of sight, or mostly, now.
Late summer afternoons! You know what I mean...."

You know what I mean, said Billy, raising up
his crippled hand to mop away the sweat
his vision brought. Many times he said it:
"You know what I mean," he'd ask or state. I nodded.
He carried on: "The first thing that I saw
when I woke up was that a star was out.

"And it was cool. I figured—I still do—
I stood as good a show as any neighbor
to get to paradise. Maybe I'd died!
That's what I thought. I even started looking
out for May. (She was the better half,
no doubt about it. She knew the bushes and flowers,

"she knew how much I missed the sheep and pastures.)
I watched a string of Blackduck settle in
on Wagner's beaver pond. A little weasel
was getting set for winter: already he wore
his high white socks. I heard that pretty thrush
you hear at dusk when there isn't any breeze.

"You see, I wasn't churchly, but I thought
if heaven's worth the breath the preachers use,
it'll be just like your life was at its best.
You've heard how people say, 'I pinched myself.'
By God, I did! To see if things would change.
When I sat up, that little weasel dove,

"but otherwise things looked about the same.
It brought back maybe half a dozen times
in life when things go on, but seem so right
you think they'll go forever with no harm.
The times I've had like that were at the farm,
when I'd be working hard all day, my mind

"hard on the job—whatever: digging, shearing—
and then I'd stop and turn, and everything
was in its place, and had a kind of shine.
You couldn't help but want to speak or sing.
Some kind of thanks, I guess. I'm not for church,
I said, but there you are.
                         I sat and watched

"the ridges. They kept swallowing the light,
all that white and yellow going blue.
I've always loved that business. I still do...."
    And Billy loved to talk, and as he wandered,
the hills took on the look that he described,
as if his words were sorcery,

as if the winter were summer, and moon were sun,
and far from being short, the Old Year's day
would last forever.
                    "There was, and I admit it,
Billy said, "some bounce now in my toes.
A lot more than before, and I made time.
And not because poor Mark was in that hole.

"By Jesus, Judge, I'll say it! I felt good.
Is that what killed Mark dead? You know it isn't.
For all I know, the boy was long since gone.
But I went on until I came to Cammon's.
I knocked the door till Elsie finished peeking
through the curtains and finally opened up.

"I knew her all my life. I meant to speak,
for all the good it ever would have done.
Elsie liked to gab, but she had no phone,
no more than I did. I don't know too much,
but I know it takes a telephone right here
to ring another there. I meant to speak.

"Before I got a word in, though, she chirped,
'Nice evening, Billy.' Just what I was thinking....
Go on and live to be an older fool
than Billy, Judge. You'll never know the way
I mean that, and you'll likely curse me too.
She came out on the step. We turned around

"and watched the bullbats worrying the bugs.
We saw the moon hike overtop The Bald Man.
You see it from your house. You know the one?"
    How could Fields think this was information?
That mountain is the first thing that you see.
And yet when Billy named a thing for me,

I'd listen, as if hearing Revelation.
For forty years, The Bald Man's been the same.
The summer folks don't put their houses there!
Its giant granite dune commands the air,
and summer or winter, complements the moon
that wanders over it.
                "We talked a spell

"in Elsie's rooms. We talked about the town
when we were young, the way it was back then—
pastures; fences; sheep. These scrubby woods
grew up when farmers couldn't make a go.
Their sons went to the city, or joined the army,
or shot their bolts out slaving with machines.

"We talked about all that before I told her
that Mark was lying out beneath her cow.
I haven't breathed a word about this, Judge,
though poor old Elsie Cammon died soon after,
and may God bless her! though she lied and said
she tried to move me on, but I was stubborn.

"Judge, she *smiled*. 'Billy, you ain't magic.'
That's the words she used. And that's the point.
It wasn't that I never meant to go
and raise some help. The better neighbor figures
all the walking played out Billy's mind.
But Judge, I'll tell you, I felt right as rain.

"We sat and drank another cup together,
and talked about the weather. Little things,
like people do. And when I thought of Mark
down in that grave, I thought for all of us
there comes a time, and maybe this is his.
And sat there happy, Judge, between us two,

"that it was his, not mine. Now that's all wrong,
because a man gets just so many years,

and I'd used up a better share of them
than Mark had done. And so I should have died
out by that tree, for that way Mark would live.
And that way, when his brothers came to fetch him,

"his blood would jump back in him from the ground,
and Elsie's cow would fly clean up to heaven,
and Elsie's fence would always be tight-strung,
and that choker apple never would have grown,
because old Fields had gone before his time,
and Blainville would be better than it was—

"the sheep would all come back and browse the hills,
the big old barns would still be up and plumb,
there'd be a foot of soil on every pasture,
and no one would go marching off to war,
and all our men and women would love forever...."
    I stopped him there. The old man's sweat was pouring

off his skin and down the tumbled bedclothes,
the way mine does sometimes.
                         But not tonight.
Tonight, recording this for you and you
—outsider, native, woman, man or child—
but mostly for myself, as I've confessed,
I'll lie here with my story, cool, a while.

A little time, while the moon plays on The Bald Man,
I'll hold to it, and you can judge the rest.

AT THE EDGE

RIVERFRONT

Savannah's purposeful pulp mills stink and labor
all night and through the weekend.
Saturday now. A bad wind.
A gang of seven skinheads seems to ponder
breaking the glass
of a shop that sells old clothes
that are suddenly in.
Camouflage and khaki are the trend.
But they lumber off.
Perhaps they'll just kick ass.

And the cars of young men
—soldiers, lucky on furlough,
millhands lucky to draw the day shift—
pass, and pass, and pass
in the night. The rotten egg odors of sulfur mix
with their racketing exhaust.
Each radio, tuned to just below
the point where speakers blow,
to the funky black station
or the murderous Heavy Metal —

each blares and clashes
with the others. Mad, impatient,
the young men gun their throttles.
One wonders if such rankness and chaos
are to the driven furious
boys a virtue.
If they think about matters like virtue.

The prosperous tourists
have taken cover in their hotels.
I'll join them now. I'm getting on. I must be.

O America. You might as well
set tanks or tigers free
in the crowded dark, I think.
Now fast-food waitresses tense, close ranks
as they make thier way home over littered sidewalks.
The young men crane their necks, roar, ache for sex.
Nothing, again, will happen, but if it did
—if on such a road
the loud boys could be satisfied,
what would their satisfaction be?

Getting on. I must be.
A black in a shabby drab jacket
holds up his sign morosely
to indifferent traffic
at the street's darkened end.
He has passed, it seems, beyond anger:
I NEED SOME WORK. PLEASE!
The collapsing margins of his paper flutter
with the poisoning wind.

UPCOUNTRY SPEEDWAY

Each of us strangely anxious   my daughter and I
driving here   in line   on this unseemly
road   nothing more than a logging trail
reclaimed   our windows down   though this is the final
evening   the last heroics   September already
already a chill from the glacier   Stars   How small
ahead   what we agree to call a roar
Second growth all but erases the babble
of revving race-car engines   by local agreement
restricted to minimal power   six cylinders stock

Not of recent manufacture   All
will be buried in dust   Minuscule town and track
1/4 mile on the outside lane   Young girlfriends
or wives cluster by village   Orient   Linneus
Wytopitlock   wide spots in the tarmac
We have our tickets   We hear the women cheer
men called Wayne or Brian   in suits emblazoned
with names   their own   their sweethearts'   sponsors'
Beauty's the female feature   frailest beauty
poised to cede itself to creases of worry

At money   fat   booze   an odd lump under
the Dacron   maybe a bruise   One prays   One swears
at her lover's rival   is joined   rebutted   insulted
Cheating's   the standard slander   Some men joke
waiting to race in the pits   Their children race
each other   boys and girls   down the grandstand
ramps or   older   betray themselves by screaming

abuse at the opposite sex or   older still
stroll toward trees   backseats   It's the final heat
Labor Day   *Gentlemen start your engines*

The official leans from his rickety tower   The green
flag flutters   At length our cries are lost
in the whine and protest of twenty badly used
autos careening toward the final turn
A few along the way appear to have broken
off the dirt   but No one ever gets hurt
So says a tiny grandma seated beside me
*You can trust your car to the man who wears
the star* stitched on her shirt   Her words are part
reassurance   it seems   and part lament

How few are satisfied   The factions shriek
dissatisfaction at the Nova that orbits
the circuit half-speed   trailing the checkered pennant
of the victor   Women   bitter   gather belongings
Wrecks are hauled away   We follow the throng
Beside us   up on a father's shoulders   a child
of uncertain gender calls out   the ancient tease
No one can get me   My own child's breaths are mist
against the mountain   under the chilly heavens
They mingle with exhalations from dark coupe's

IN THE ALLEY

Vague airs remain, I guess, of some classical time
        even in modern Florence.
And so, trailing the beat of his cane on stone, the blind
        man just now in the alley
among the Vespas, Fiats, gawking tourists—
        he or his blindness made me
think of my highschool role as Greek Oedipus,
        and of painfully lisping through
        lines like "Why do you strew
yourselves before these altars with supplications?"

        Girls close to the stage
nudged each other when I butchered a word like *Thebes*.
        More shyness in me than rage,
save at a Fate that hampered articulation;
        but I knew what it was to despise
oneself, and maybe learned something of grief
        after I'd stabbed my eyes
with the brooch I'd yanked from the breast of Bonnie Lester,
        so credible as Jocasta,
her unspectacled face tense. (She was badly myopic.)

        This was when Marlon Brando's
method with Method was all I longed to mimic;
        I held my lids tight-closed
until the lights were cut and the curtain fell.
        (Just now I watched him pause,
the blind man, light a pipe, profoundly inhale.
        I stopped in the alley and saw....)

It must have been some twenty full minutes of darkness,
        deep in its way as sleep,
deep as the womb. I yet can smell the greases,

        crimson on either cheek,
the sweat in my bedsheet toga, the drugstore perfume
        on my kneeling, wailing children.
And other more troubling things: just as my tongue
        thickly delivered its burdens,
sounds conspired within that musty gym
        that, sighted, I hadn't discovered:
the tobacco cough of my dad (it would do him in);
        the stagehands' snickers
(they were jocks who had elective requirements to fill);

        the rustle of cloth, so piquant
on Antigone's shoulders: she was my fan, that girl,
        and she and I had flirted,
though I'd told Jocasta I loved her more than the world.
        Surely it wasn't true,
but I fantasized too that I heard my mother mouthing
        the lines she had led me through,
and heard her scold my father out of his dozing....
        Just now I tried it over;
I let my lids come down.... But pigeons exploding

        under my feet, and the odors
of street and wall, the haggle of merchants, the snarl
        of scooter and car in their bustling—
in this my exile terrified me all.
        Before the perilous crossing,

where I'd thought to help the blind man cross the street,
    after awkwardly rehearsing
the offer I'd make in that half-learned classic speech,
    I'd looked away. Now
he levelled his cane and fared out into the square.

    I searched for him in the crowd,
saw nothing but a slip of smoke on air.

SPITE: HER TALE

Someone else would tell a different version:

There was a tree, a twisty beech, out back,
no earthly use, not even for a shade.
You know the way of a tree in this cold place:
it starts a hefty trunk, and then the winds
and winters grind at it, the tightwad earth
will starve it till it almost seems to send
branches sideways-out to look for friends.

I recollect that beech's early years:

Mighty plans, just as I said, to start,
which it would drop in time ... but first it tried
somehow to sneak its way to being tall:
at three feet high, it took a funny swerve,
headed south a year or two, and then
came back in line to make a loop, or bow.
After that, it grew just anyhow.

Where it curved, it left a sort of seat.

I've made a loop myself. I'll start again.
My Harry's lights went out about when mine did.
I never saw them lay him down, just heard
the diggers grunt, the clods and gravel tumble,
the frost-clumps fall in too, the frozen sods.
Then came the spring, so quick you thought it couldn't.
Our Buck got done with school and married Susan,

and she moved here to run the farm with him.

We say The Farm, though Harry didn't die
the way I guess he should have —flinging hay,
or pulling calves, or mucking out a stall.
He fell among old tire irons and ratchets,
his cutting torch on fire, a snakey tailpipe
hung at him from a Ford up on the hoist,
the muffler shop's blue fumes too much at last.

His heart was never what it should have been.

Buck claims he's added two head to the herd.
I know better. I can hear the truth.
And after all, I lived here all those years
with both my eyes. I never say a thing.
He works a night job, cleaning up a morgue.
Not that I judge— a farmer nowadays
does what he must to help the farm get by.

What I want to talk about is spite:

or maybe I should call it cruelty.
It doesn't matter anyway. Just words.
Now understand me. I'm not out for pity.
No one ever hit me or abused me,
though I've got just enough imagination
to picture it, the old man coming home,
a half a case in him, and feeling down.

Bad pay and bills ... but she's the one to suffer,

to get beat up for nothing that she's done.
Thing is, I think I know how *he* feels too;
the world's a funny place, make no mistake.
Buck and Sue would likely tell this different,
but even I don't say the word *abused*.
Back to the tree... but first let me confess
that at the start I fairly was a mess:

I moped and whined, a lot more than I should have,

but I'd been never one to stand around
with people waiting on me—I could do it!—
and never thought how much I used my eyes,
how much I'd taken pleasure from my sight.
(You know the saying: "You don't miss your water....")
Don't get me wrong: I don't mean watching things
they dream make women purr in magazines—

rising dough, the patterns in a quilt.

If I looked at such stuff, I had plain reasons:
a person has to feed and warm herself.
When I say sight, I mean a person's hands—
the way they'll spread or clamp or pick or fiddle;
or, when you look straight into it, a face—
its grins, its grimaces and in-betweens.
A cloud. A track. A brook. A mink. A tree.

I liked a busyness that wanted eyes,

just like poor Harry: how it sickens me
to think he spent his last years tinkering
and twisting screws. He wasn't made for that.
I had to dig down somewhere for a will;
I had to figure I could sit and rot,
and wreck the children's lives into the bargain,
or I could somehow, someway get a move on.

And so I did. I learned to watch with ears.

It's not that I saw much, but what I saw
I saw as clear as any sighted person.
I think that once I started it came easy
because, when I'd had eyes, I'd kept an eye out....
But let me get back to that twisty tree,
the one thing that I came to know the best,
the thing that helped me locate all the rest.

Every day, no matter what the weather,

I'd get myself out to it, settle in,
my backside and my back a perfect fit
inside the bow or loop I've spoken of.
I wore that cranny's bark smooth where I sat,
and where I lay my hands was smooth as well.
I saw things when the beech would creak with wind,
or even when an owl came to a limb.

In peace or torment, I could see the tree.
When squirrels squabbled on a higher branch,
when nuts plopped on the ground, if there were nuts,
when winter redpolls, siskins, chickadees
would come or go, or leather-colored leaves
that hang tight through the snows would flap and click:
I'd mark the sound and piece the tree together
(for all I know I got it wrong. I never

paid that beech much mind till I was blind).

And once I fitted out the shape again,
then I could see the farm; and once I saw
the farm, the cows or steers or calves, whatever,
then I felt I knew where I belonged
in all this universe ... and all because
I'd noticed squirrels, leaves, a breeze, a bird.
All because I saw what I had heard,

and thought, and listened hard to what I thought.

In fact I came to see the tree much better
than even I saw Harry in my mind;
in fact I came to think of it as Harry,
a funny thing—there wasn't any reason:
I can't recall him speak of it at all
when he was living. It's the way I said:
it didn't even make a decent shade.

I never spoke a word about all this,

no solitary word to Buck or Susan
on what the tree's idea had come to mean—
not as you might guess that I was scared
they'd laugh at me for loving some old beech.
I wasn't sure for one thing it was love,
at least not for the tree. I couldn't say
just what it was. And so I didn't say.

But I had changed. There wasn't any doubt.

You know, it seemed that Buck and Sue preferred
when I was ugly—quick to snap, or cry.
Some people like you better broken down;
then all they think they have to do is tinker
with you like a gear. But understand:
I'm no philosopher; I'm not inclined.
I'll let you explain, if you've a mind,

the way they acted. Here it is, I think:

right before my eyes, they cut that tree
and sawed it up for cordwood. Now that's spite!
You can't just chop away a thing like that.
They claimed that all its branches had gone dead,
but I of course knew better, knew that tree
as well as my own soul, and I still do.
Did they mean for me to have no place to go?

Here it is. I keep it right inside.

It's hard to say what they keep. Cruelty—
I never feel a craving to return it.
They won't have any kids, although God knows
I don't claim that's the last bad fate God dreamed.
I had a child, and where did I come out?
I came out sitting up a tree, they'd say.
I know—they don't—just what that means to me.

Buck cleans dead men's dust from dark till dawn.

I stay alone on weekend nights. They dance
down in a place so full of lights it blinds,
or so they say (and turn their laughter mean)—
a place that blinds, a band that plays so loud
they can't hear what they say or even think.
I know the things I know. I nod and rock.
I never feel the need to pay them back.

AT THE EDGE
—*Monte Tremezzo*

Runaway limestone, snow, ghost of a path.
Losing my reckless footing, there I hung,
if just for a moment. What do they say of the drowned?
Their lives leap up entire and eddy past.
For me, high over the lake, it was lyrics of songs:
"Getting to Know You," "Work Song," "Jazz-Me Blues,"
these and others whose words have nothing to do
with anything I've lived, or any place.
Bright spoils, that's all, of a far too passive lifetime:
in one ear but not quite out the other.
At the edge in all abundance they floated to mind.

Once I built an airplane for my daughter,
slapped it together with remnant shingles and nails.
Crude as it was, she loved it. Stuff for tears—
how little she asks, how little I give. I failed
to think of her then, of the plane unsuited to flight
as much as I. Nor did I think up there
of the older son to whom I've offered advice
I scarcely follow myself; I've spoken of working,
of discipline, dedication. Nor of my wife,
who struggled and bore our ten-months' boy, and nursed him,
the one who fought just then at home to stand,
to speak in a room I'd left behind for a season
that I might cross the ocean and rove these mountains.

My head a concert hall for some great band
whose tin-pan scraps of history were playing:

"Satin Doll," "I've Got the World on a String," "I'm Just Biding My Time," "Pennies from Heaven." Below, abroad, people were living, learning, laboring, raising the young. I dreamt my songs.

ROAD AGENT

When the sun rises, they get them away
and lie down in their dens.
Man goes forth to his work
and to his labor until the evening.
—*Ps. 104*

It doesn't seem so cursed in summer.
If a job could ever turn sweet, that's when.
There's just a little brush to tend.
Or I cuff the washboard flat with the grader.

You don't even have to swat the flies.
Diesel-smoke and noise will drive them.
The best is, I can look to the mountain!
The seat will raise a man that high.

The plow's high, too, but you can't look off.
Sun-up to sun-down, eyes on the road.
The mountain's still there when it goes cold.
But in winter you have to mind yourself.

Your help will quit you sure as Judas.
I clear the ice and snow on my own.
Everyone seems to go to den.
Kiss them good-bye when the weather freezes.

They call on the town or move to the city.
It's soft, but it isn't by Jesus my way.
I'm not like the state boys out on the highway.
I don't despise what isn't easy.

I'm what I was made, and nothing else.
I mean to earn my bread by sweat.
Foolish, the things that some expect.
God helps them that help themselves.

Some can't dream why I'd keep at it.
No matter, what this one and that one say.
They vote me back on town meeting day.
But the new folks' notions and mine are different.

(The oldtimers don't much like to talk.
I do it for them—I'm elected.
It comes with the work, and I guess it's expected.)
The newcomers squawk and I squawk back.

First thing to do, they say, is the schoolyard.
They have to get at the books, those kids!
(True, it's what my mother said.
The times would pass me by, she figured.)

But someone should bless the poor in school.
Everyone better not turn out bright.
They do, and these roads close down tonight.
They could own the world and lose their souls.

That's in a book, and makes some sense.
I graduated with less than I brought.
Of course I started going with Hat.
You couldn't call it a total loss.

We've kept on going, with six good children.
Say *that* for some that study college.
Say they got *that* out of all their knowledge.
Say they got it from education.

Last week I was working Sutter's Knoll.
I came on poor young Mrs. Grayson.
She had this little flimsy dress on.
You'd judge she was out for a summer stroll.

Her husband's diplomas would fill a trunk.
(Half-bare, she was, in a foot of snow!
I pretended a wing was loose on the plow.)
He's one of those jacket-and-necktie drunks.

Town Hall's the next that's got to be done.
The politicians insist on that.
They're damned important, you can bet.
I guess I oughtn't to run them down.

They hang on tougher than lots of others.
Take what few are left in The Grange.
It seems so quick, the way it's changed!
There aren't that many around to remember.

Things were different here one time.
The Grange is ready to fall on the ground.
Who cares nowadays in town?
I do it early, all the same.

Let them fire me: I've lived through worse.
It wasn't Happily-Ever-After.
It wasn't Everyone-Love-Your-Neighbor.
And the good Lord knows the money was scarce.

Then I plow the American Legion Post.
(There was always a battle or two somewhere.)
Schooling, politics and war.
Father, Son, and Holy Ghost.

I'm not even supposed to do the church.
That road is twisty, even in light.
I wait and fuss with it in the night.
Taxpayer money — they'd moan and bitch.

Dead last, this house of God out here.
But He says from the mountain, The last will be first.
In the end He says, The first'll be last.
This is the one I fight to get clear.

The hardest one, in the cold of the year.

REVISION: EARLY DECEMBER

You didn't pay the price.
His old rebuke rises in after-dinner calm,
fireplace glow grown general in the room,
my armchair stalwart. Joys of the commonplace
collide in dream with rank, ammoniac
odors—muddy jersey, yellowed
headband—and a scent like the stains of sex:
grass at abraded knee and elbow.

Coach chops the air with brutal hand and baits us.
Are we deaf and dumb? He wants to know.
Men or babies, girls or boys? Oh, how
can we respond? He looms above us
and the drafts of defeat
that rise from our downflung frames
at which he spits
his imbecile slogans. We've lost the game,

but winning is not the important thing, as he has it
(quoting an even crueler idiot);
it's the only thing. How can we bear
his contempt for simple joy
into the shower? There, in an ordinary hour,
the wetted smacks would sound
of towel and hand—
the mirthful aggressions of boys

who needn't reckon yet what life entails.
How can I bear it home, where in the mail
has come the news of early admission
to college, which ought to be sufficient
to qualify this sullenness and torpor?
I seal my fat lips all through dinner,
but for a sip of juice that sears their wounds.
I clench the purpled eyes that lust to disburden

themselves before father and mother, sisters, brothers.
I still can feel it: silence like fog,
and I within it, cursing the bones,
the very bones, of Coach's jaw—like a hog's;
the bull neck at the root of a blunted skull;
the elephantine calves that bulge
his everlasting sweatpants; the other bulge
(so clearly a badge of station) where trunk thighs meet.

I curse each inch, forgetting in my hate
to include the simian hands with which he'll make
signs tonight to his idiot child.
In the shower stall, the laundry hangs.
Remains of supper congeal on Willoware plates.
A heater labors. His wife sorts bills
on her narrow bed. The slumping son attends
sign after sign. Coach lusts for them to prevail.

INSOMNIA: THE DISTANCES

     Cliché can be true: You hate to open the paper
and read that someone stood,
         as dumb as wood,
     while a big truck knocked the plain hell out of her daughter
the morning after the party, as the child tried out
     her birthday bike. You can almost hear a lot
of scrambled sounds, and then the terrible quiet.
     Speaking of hell, how about the roar

     of air and people for thousands of feet before
the doomed plane crashes?
         Vacation clothes—madras,
     pastel, batik—bleed together, swear.
Bunches of people! Or the other scores that go down
     under official or unofficial guns
every day. Boom! Somebody's done,
         done in again— wiped out, dispatched. Or else

     just thrown back on him-or-her Self
by bad news; illness; violence:
         nothing but silence,
     except for tick and tock from a bedroom shelf,
or maybe the kitchen fridge's strange little moan,
     or wires way out on the road—*click hum*—
like a too-hard-driven car as it cools down.
     Or a roofbeam groans. Maybe an apple falls,

     thump! on the lawn. Even that may cause
a person to muse:
      something can fall on you.
   Don't feel safe because it never has.
"In this life, you'd better by God trust nothing" :
    that's what I heard from a man of apparent learning,
in a cramped bar. (The Optimists were meeting
     in the main room.) As if there were somehow

    another life. That was real. He knew.
I don't know how he knew it,
     but you could *see* it—
maybe in the way his bull neck bowed,
and the way he couldn't manage to keep the stammer
    out of his talk; his hands were like 8-pound hammers,
but they shook on his mug of beer. An end to the matter:
     that single comment. Then silence. Don't believe

    each and every thing you happen to read,
they say. All well-and-good,
     but when you-know-what
   has hit the fan for someone you can see ....
That's different, and maybe then you begin to hear
    something behind what you read, like the indistinct words
of a far-off song.   Don't ask me, How can we care
    about someone or something we don't even know?

Listen to things. Color them in. Like so:
Somebody's saddened,
>> she wants to know what'll happen—
> charity's failing because the economy's slow.
What of a worthy cause like the Animal Shelter?
> I came on these worries a while back in a letter
to the editor: it could have been written better,
>> but here that isn't my particular worry.

> *She* cares, though—about the kittens and puppies...
"Where will they turn?"
>> I'm afraid by now she's learned:
> Down. So think of her. Maybe she fancies
a tricolor male, a "money cat," or a Manx.
> Something rare. A weird mutt, a mix
of skinny Bluetick hound and pedigreed Spitz,
>> and so the pup has the nailkeg head of a Husky

on top of a long-leg, racehorse body,
with markings by Heinz:
>> 57 stripes
> and spots. Or just a common pooch or tabby,
and all they do, and all she does, is whine.
> She can't speak, just lets the tears run down
till all are asleep. Common or garden pain:
>> The child's hair was yellow, the bike was green,

                    the sky was gray.... Was.   That great big man,
the one at the bar:
                    he was himself, sure,
                but also anybody whose life turns mean
as hell—maybe someone got shot, maybe
                    something burned down; it's the end, maybe,
of a love they thought would last forever; or he
                    —or needless to say it could be she—was

                    supposed to be in the best of health. Was.
Supposed.   There I was
                    myself, supposed
                to be having the time of my life inside the walls
of this ruined Italian village. Quaint. Hell!
                no newspaper, books, not even any mail
to read for weeks.   I still can't tell
                    what it was: the tick of my little alarm?

                    an animal's cry? Maybe a truck-tire's boom ,
or a jet's; or a fridge that squeaked;
                    or a rafter that creaked.
                Was someone somewhere singing a drunken song?
Or was it just this terrible quiet in the room,
                and outside too?—Nothing. Not a peep.
And I woke up, and thought, and wrote this down,
                    in the night, in a tiny, silent, faraway town.

                    And now it seems a hell of a distance to sleep.

THE HITCH-HIKER

He speaks as if I knew him: "Mr. Troop will feed him.
I'll be right back. The dog understands.
See him roll over, shake hands.
      I like all my animals:
now *they* was horses!—Dusky, Dan....

"Cavalry. '29:
I'm going down after that pension of mine.
A man's got something coming by 75.
      I married the Rutland girl—
the sight of her! Remember? Man alive!

"Enough to cause a horse to eat his bedding!
Me at Pratt and Whitney, weaving
wire from dawn to dusk, all day.
      How'd you like to come on home,
and she's seen someone else or three?

"Women want their bellies full.
I showed her the road, I guess you recall.
I told her, 'Don't look back.'
      Like a dog: don't care who gets it done.
'Don't look back.'

"Roll completely over,
give you a kiss, remember?
but how could I take him on the road?
      Mr. Troop will feed him.
Always a friendly boy, like you....

"You know what happened to the second wife.
A horse, a rifle....
our youngest boy, after all we done.
      Fairly honest, decent.
You haven't forgot she used to be a nun.

"Nose and ears! By Jesus, how they bled her!
You couldn't find a better.
That boy, and the way she brooded!
      The Gaysville Town Clerk's fairly honest.
'Go visit her, up the mountain,' they recommended.

"But she knows who run down my son.
Just giving me the dance-around.
The blood came out the nose and ears, all black.
      She fussed on him. Hard enough, them moments,
and wouldn't give my driver's license back.

"A Polack's horsed around, more than his share,
by the time he's beaten back this many years.
I was going to the dances with a Catholic girl,
      and me a Mason!
She finds out, and it's 'Here's the Devil!'

"Can you beat such a damned thing?
My niece got the ring:
two diamonds, and some other stone—blue.
      I ain't heard from her since the time of Creation.
I bet she's seeing someone else or two.

"See them parading at Pratt: the bagpipes! bells!
By God I've had a bellyfull,
but you just get blue if you keep looking back.
      Jesus! I *had* to be a Mason!
They all was Scots, McThis-and-That.

"But just the same as we would, pledge the flag.
Before your time: that was the good old gang!
And me the Devil! 'Kiss me!'
      That's what I said. I wasn't—
Jesus! what the hell?—I wasn't dirty.

"You could weave wire all day all dressed in white.
A while since you've seen him, but he's still white
as a diamond right through mud-time.
      Takes food right out of your mouth.
Stands up, parades around.

"Rolls over, gives you a kiss, begs for that food,
speak to you if he could.
All Scotch, but spoke the pledge like me.
      Had to. Pratt didn't take no guff.
What the hell? Good company.

"Are you from around? He waits for me all day.
I feed old Dusky and Dan when Troop's away."
And so again I'm the stranger: "You couldn't find a better.
      He doesn't have a wife or woman.
The pup will understand. He owes me the favor.

"He has a swelling on his head,
or I wouldn't brood and fuss so.
My name is Eugene Botch.
      Come visit. Up the mountain.
I know to you it might sound English or Scotch,

"but I'm a Polack, really.
It's really 'Boteszeski.'
We won't be wanting good company.
      I'll show you one or two girls.
A Cavalryman will have them handy.

"Visit. I'll be there. Just scooting down
the road to get what's coming to me now.
I'll be all right. Don't look back.
      A tough old dog. A hard old Devil.
Visit. I'll be right back."

PRIVATE BOYS' SCHOOL, 3RD GRADE

Teacher is like every woman, of course—
a "Mrs." Lives in a storybook house
Of whitest clapboard. Dick and Jane and Spot

Her dog will greet her after school gets out.
That's our joke. We see them all on a lawn
Of unspoiled grass, each shrub well planned, well pruned.

Soon she puts her satchel down in the hall
And does her rounds: fills up Spot's dish with meal,
Makes Janie's doll as neat as new again.

Maybe Dick is a less-than-perfect son,
Scolded like us for failed marks and manners.
"Wash up," she chides, then has him add figures

On paper clean as we can only dream.
Or so we hope, while Mr. Grady beams
Satisfaction at the roast in gravy,

Centered in the oven. Mrs. Grady
Strikes a match at last and holds it over
Every candle, tiny flame that hovers,

A momentary but punctilious dot
Above each flawless i . She may or not
Wear a ring, a thing outside our notice.

Once, a fearful downpour comes upon us,
Unlike the placid weathers in our books,
And as she herds us, slickered, to the bus,

The wind upfurls our Mrs. Grady's dress.
We glimpse rent stockings, rolled beneath blue knees;
Some wiseguy says, sophisticatedly,

"See Mrs. Grady's runs!" But she can't hear.
And then the cold, the gloomy time of year—
Light gets slight, and labor more obnoxious:

Subordinates, qualifiers, commas.
Even more sternness in the way we're taught;
She says strange things like "Every sentence ought

To hold together now. Your stories have
To be real stories, rounded out, like life."
How we grimace, our tongues between our teeth,

At noun and predicate that won't agree,
At run-on phrase, question mark forgotten.
All our story-notions come up rotten.

Term snaps shut. She claps us to her bosom,
Hotly, each in turn. She makes us kiss her,
Whimper, scarlet-eared, how much we'll miss her,

Though there's not one who doesn't feel distaste,
If only at her tear-bespattered face:
Has she not spent these months upbraiding us

Like ornery dogs for smears and tears and blots,
For "sloppiness," which showed we "planned badly"?
"These can spoil your lives," said Mrs. Grady.

BLACK BEAR CUFFING FOR FOOD

After the leaf-lookers' season, I'm alone
on the road to watch his labor.
> Time of the spendthrift maple,
> frost-burned fern,
> ripe riverside butternuts splashing
> into the water and gone.

Time by God to get set,
as he appears already to have learned,
> dark shoulders, rhythmic, heaving
> back and forth, back and forth,
> and in the rests,
> hand to mouth, hand to mouth.

He looks a little like Mongo Santamaria
rapt above the dried hide of his conga,
> thumping out "Watermelon Man,"
> memory I wrest
> from some gone nightclub cellar,
> thick with a general gray smoke.

Now halfway down
the hills in the dusk air's chill,
> it's cloud that is gray and thick.
> A wonder, the mind's autonomy—
> or enslavement.... I smile to recall Mongo's drum,
> and over its crackle and pop the horns' glissandi.

I play them back in mind, alone
at the edge of Macalister's field,
> where a young bear cuffs for ants in latest October.
> The work is for scant return
> and however furious, slow.
> Soon, sleep, at whose muddy far end will be hunger.

I mean for all these signs to mean:
I imagine how, come spring, a rusty stalk,
> missed in the reaping,
> will show here and there in the rows;
> and a scrap of someone's shirt-tail or frock,
> on barbed wire next to the lane.

For now, the bear is disappearing
into the twilight and fog,
> into the time
> of glowing jackolanterns without measure
> beneath the colored corn that hangs in windows.
> Now children study the rags they'll turn into costumes.

And I, who've merely ridden to the grocery store,
will start again
> back through woods in their final flames.
> Past the pond where sometimes for pleasure
> I flick a bright fly for fish I let go,
> and down the neat gravel drive, beyond the door,

> my family waits. It's supper time.
> Down in the islands bright melons are a staple.
> How exotic it seems, and oh,
> and oh how colorful....

WYOMING

The lives one stumbles into and over!
For him, they were figured everywhere—
even here, in a personless prairie
that bedded a snaky-sinuous river.

Feeling smug, responsible, righteous,
he unhooked and freed a big brown trout,
then for respite staggered out
of the current. Under the cutbank's bushes

he kicked a slackwater: black-nosed daces
bolted in panic, re-grouped and bolted.
Intrusion on peace became a theme
for the man, who'd stood so blithe mid-stream,

at one with his world, he thought. Revolted,
he grunted onto the bank. Bull elk
all morning long had yodelled their longings,
yet now their bugles sounded like warnings,

loud but oblique, that any boy
might hear from his elders. Loathing his bulk,
his grizzled mug, his absence of grace,
he muttered, *Deliver , deliver me...* ,

until a visionary face
showed on the water—both angry and anxious,
and somehow female, it split into features
which scattered and grouped and scattered, like fishes.

Life struck the man as all synchronic....
Racing a flabby marmot holeward,
a buteo screamed, and swooped, and won.
The bird was dark, and fierce, and phallic.

The Prophet says there is nothing new
for us to study under the sun,
which just now dazed each gout of dew,
and bloodied it, so he surmised.

He'd kill the next good trout to rise.
He might as well....   'Hoppers and duns
rattled or fluttered as noon arrived;
some lit on the surface to drown, or be eaten.

He hadn't intended to press his rough track
on the minnows' pool as he left the river,
nor did he mean in coming hither
to crush the fragile sages' necks,

et cetera. These things just happened,
no one to blame. Or so he reasoned.
Two bulls now clashed their dangerous racks.
And he kept vaguely praying, *Deliver,*

Deliver , O deliver me....
So he would pray for many a season:
Deliver this heavy-gaited boy
into—or was it out of?— nature.

IN THE BLIND
—for Tommy White, my oldest friend

As in water face answers to face, the Proverb says,
so the mind of man reflects the man ...
which must in my case mean the surface is roiled
as this one before me when it's lashed by furious beavers.
What a lot of time I spend in the blind,
splashing from thought to thought,
moving at random.
And how often I reach for you,
we shared so much, we rode all over God's acre
together, and always thought the same.
Now that we shoot toward fifty,

what does it all add up to?
Quick birds that breast the sun and rob my breath;
the revelation of internal pattern
in a fireplace log
at the moment my axe lays it open,
before I throw it on the heap
to dry, to be burned. Whiffs of memory.
Is the beautiful random enough?
Everything that is here and must go away.
(I wonder if you have time
for all this stuff.)

Sometimes late in November,
the river will suddenly turn austere, abstract,
as if its waves would cease their movement, stiffen.
Maybe you remember
how we used to argue over religion.
Especially in the fall,

it seems I still expend a lot of my life
waiting for something to light beside me and stay.
How often I'll be here,
the marsh alive around me
—something that riffles the slue, a rustle in weeds—

but the sky so empty only thought can fill it.
Except for the slow-motion stars. And except for Queen Moon:
just this morning, perfectly round,
she still was high, and my thought was of you
one time when you offered me a confession,
and it was hard,
for we thought of ourselves as rock-hard adolescents.
"Sometimes," you said, "I could cry
when I hear that Christmas carol,
'O Little Town of Bethlehem.'"

I laughed. I know exactly what you mean,
though we don't anymore have much in common
except this past that speaks to us in symbols
—the important part, at least—
and usually mutely.
It's that part about the deep and dreamless sleep,
am I right?
That, and the way the silent stars go by.
I think I knew even then what I feel now,
however hard of expression.
This morning, I say, the moon was full,

and there I was, half-asleep,
in my ignorance waiting for some wondrous declension,
the advent of ... what?

There are moments in the blind
when I could simply lay back my head and bellow.
Do you remember those summer evenings
in your father's Rocket 88
when we'd fly back and forth like swallows
trapped in a building?
Here to there to there to here!
And yet we felt ourselves free,

the radio loud, loudly singing along.
Remember the Dells' old anthem?
"O, What a Night."
We didn't know where we were going,
but everything on the way was so perfectly lovely
—the silent little towns winking like planets,
the rolling frost-studded country—
moment to moment to moment,
what could it matter?
Over the undulant doo-wop, that falsetto.
Something also that hovered above us,

at least we thought so.
Some ever-available charm. I yet can see,
as if they were caught in a mirror,
our heads thrown back in song,
eyes to the sky,
improvising harmony, light like a symbol
of something up there, sure and answerable.
Possible, undivided, great.
As if we were not moving at all.
Streaming down on each kindred face,
a light like grace.

WEDDING ANNIVERSARY
— for MRB

Even past sunrise, frog-legions peeped in spring
where—as if for him—the creek jagged near.
And yet from dawn, from spring, something was missing.
There were quartzes and pyrites and schists and mica plates
on the opposite scarp. They'd crackle. He would stir
the backpool's gathered algae with a stick
till the world spun in a vortex that contained
lights, quicksilver minnows, verdigris newts.
And after, reflected riverside trees would shiver,
their birds odd lapidary fruit that sang.
His awkward schoolroom recitations seemed
an age away. And yet there was something missing.

The stars above the pastures of adolescence
were profligate, scattered; and all the whispered words
he traded with his friends, though banal, thrilled him.
It was as if rich adulthood would take
the form of speech, as if to talk enough
to companions would be to lisp his way to treasure,
various as those stars, or the sighs and chippings
of amorous insects, nightbirds, rodents, cattle,
or summer timothy stalks, or breezes panting
warmly. He recalls how their radio crooned
"Shangrih-La," "Rags to Riches," whatever.
Rifeness was all. But there was an absence too.

Later he learned the words, the syntax, moods
of another language. Still later he found himself
high in the Pyrenees, unsponsored, free.
He had no cash, but could speak and charm no less
than *Monsieur le maire,* who accepted his draft and poured
coin from the hamlet's coffers and poured him wine.
They leaned out over a rail to see September's
shatter of water on rocks in the gorge below.
Then mayor and manchild stumbled house to house—
he remembers the musical speeches of introduction,
as if the boy himself were somehow a treasure.
Copious tears at parting, then something missing

All through the long, olfactory ramble north:
meadow-scent, soft coal, diesels' perfumes,
sawdust-and-urine whiff in the tiny *relais* ,
Gauloises, cheroots, and, once in Paris, cassis .
Liquor-courageous, he nodded to the lady.
And then, upstairs, the spirits fading, he bellowed,
to mask his shyness, "I have had enough!"
"J'en ai marre!" To which she replied, *"De quoi?"*
Mute, he handed over what money was left
from the Mayor's store, and mortified waited outside
on the balcony, its grillwork broken by light.
He thought, *"De quoi?"* Exactly. Enough of what?

Trout, platooned and hungry in western Montana,
the gilded Browns, the Rainbows more than rainbows,
the Cutthroats' cheek-plates crimson as any wound:
breaking the flawless surface, flawless themselves,
they arched their backs and sipped his little fly
with its tinsel and feather, never so lovely as they were.
Coyotes sang the sun to splendid disaster.
It fell on the rim of the mesa, imploding in flame,
across which flew the tuneful, crop-full geese
while blackhawks wheeled, while great bull elk came forth
to bugle challenge, courtship down the buttes,
which shone like mercury now. And something missing,

Something that failed as well to show from ice
outside his house, New Hampshire. Within, soft groans
from his ancient timbers. His clothing snapped with static.
One songless nuthatch lit to taste his feeder.
It seemed that nature vanished into mind,
that pool and pasture, mountain and minnow, frogs,
odors, effects of touch and sound and light
had each become mere object of recall.
The newest New Year passed and seemed not new,
but raced to retrospection, as would spring
and summer and autumn, so he thought, like winter
missing something. How could he know you

would come, and come the day of which he sings?
Has gone on singing. Will go on to sing.

THE FEUD

THE FEUD

I don't know your stories. This one here
is the meanest one *I've* got or ever hope to.
Less than a year ago. Last of November,
but hot by God! I saw the Walker gang,

lugging a little buck. (A sandwich size.
It *would* be. That bunch doesn't have the patience.
I'd passed up two no smaller, and in the end
the family had no venison that fall.)

I waved to them from the porch—they just looked up—
and turned away. I try to keep good terms
with everyone, but with a crowd like that
I don't do any more than necessary.

It wasn't too much cooler back inside.
A note from my wife on the table said the heat
had driven her and the kids to the town pond beach
to sit. That made some sense. It's the last that will.

I peeked out quick through the window as the Walkers'
truck ripped past, and said out loud, "Damn fools!"
The old man, "Sanitary Jim" they call him,
at the wheel, the rifles piled between

him and "Step-and-a-Half," the crippled son.
In back, all smiles and sucking down his beer,
"Short Jim" and the deer. Now Short Jim seems all right.
To see his eyes, in fact, you'd call him shy.

He doesn't talk quite plain. Each word sounds like
a noise you'd hear from under shallow water.
I didn't give it too much thought till later,
when the wife and kids came home, and wanted to know

what in Jesus' name that awful smell was,
over the road? Turns out that Walker crew
had left their deer guts cooking in the sun.
And wasn't that just like them? Swear to God,

to leave that mess beside a neighbor's house
for stink, and for his dogs to gobble up?
And there was one thing more that puzzled me:
why wouldn't they take home that pile of guts

to feed *their* dogs? A worthless bunch—
the dogs, I mean, as well as them. You'd think
they wouldn't be above it. Every decent
dog they ever had was bullshit luck,

since every one they run is one they stole
or mooched out of the pound. You'll see them all,
hitched to one lone post, dung to the elbows,
and every time they get themselves a new one,

he'll have to fight it out until the others
either chew him up or give him up.
I guessed I'd do this feeding for them, so
I raked up all the lights into a bag

and after nightfall strewed them in their dooryard
with a note: "Since I'm not eating any deer meat,
I'd just as quick your guts rot somewhere else
as by my house." And signed my actual name.

The whole thing's clear as Judgment in my mind:
the sky was orange, the air so thick it burned
a man out of his senses. I'm the one.
And evening never seemed to cool me off,

though I'm a man whose aim is not to truck
in such a thing. I've lost most of my churching,
but don't believe in taking up with feuds.
I usually let the Good Lord have His vengeance.

Nothing any good has ever grown
out of revenge. So I was told in school
when I slapped up Lemmie Watson, because he broke
the little mill I built down on the brook.

And so I learned. I spent the afternoons
that week indoors, and I've been different since,
till this one day. Then something else took over.
There passed a week: they stove my mailbox up.

At least I don't know who in hell beside them
would have done it. I had a spare. (The Lord
knows why.) I cut a post and put it up,
and could have left the blessed fracas there,

and would have, as my wife advised me to.
And I agreed. I told myself all night,
my eyes wide open, lying there and chewing,
"Let it go." And would have, as I claim,

but two days passed, and they came hunting coons
on this side of the ridge. I heard their hounds.
(God knows what *they* were running. Hedgehogs? Skunks?
It could have been.) Out on the porch

I heard *tick-tick*. Dog paws, and all *my* dogs
began to yap and whine. I made a light.
Shaky, thin as Satan, a docktail bitch,
a black-and-tan (almost), was looking in.

I made of her. She followed me as if
I'd owned her all my life out to the kennel.
I stuck her in the empty run that was
Old Joe's before I had to put him down.

I filled a dish with meal. She was a wolf!
The first square feed she'd had in quite a time.
My wife kept asking what I could be up to.
Likes to worry. Next day I drove clear

to Axtonbury, to the county pound.
"This dog's been hanging round my house all week.
Don't know who she belongs to." Lies, of course.
I had her collar locked in the Chevy's glovebox.

I wouldn't harm a dog unless I had to,
and figured this one stood a better show
to make out at the pound than at the Walkers'.
But the Walkers didn't know that. Driving home,

I flung the collar in their dooryard. After dark,
and spitting snow, six inches by next day,
late in December now, toward Christmas time.
Things shifted into higher gear despite me.

Or on account of me. Why not be honest?
I know that nowadays it's not the fashion
to think a person's born what he becomes;
but Sanitary Jim, his wife and family:

I never gave it too much thought but must
have figured right along that they belonged
to that great crowd of folks who *don't* belong.
Their children wear their marks right on them: speech

you hardly understand, a rock and sway
where a normal boy would take an easy stride.
And in and out of jail. If they can't find
another bunch to fight with, why, they'll fight

with one another. (Sleep with one another
too, if talk can be believed. Somehow
two homely sisters are in the mix as well.)
Short Jim beat an uncle or a cousin

—I disremember—beat him right to death.
(It's not the fashion either nowadays
to keep a violent man in jail. A month, no more,
goes by, and Short Jim's on the town again.)

But back to what I just began. The Walkers
are as bad as banty roosters, and I figured
they were meant somehow to be. Where most of us
are meant to eat one little peck of dirt,

they eat a truckload. Is it any wonder,
then, I didn't make a special point
of mixing with them? No more than I would
with any crowd that filthed itself that way.

But mix with them I did. It seemed as if
their style of working things reached up and grabbed me.
I was in the game so quick it turned my head.
The snow came on, the first big storm of winter,

that night I pulled the trick with the docktail's collar.
In the morning, barely filled, I saw their tracks
around my kennel. But *my* runs both are solid
chain-link, and the doors are padlocked shut.

They mean a thing or two to me, those dogs.
I keep the keys right on me. No one else
—no family, no good friend— can spring a dog
of mine. That way, I know they're there, or *with* me.

I'm only puzzled that they never growled. They do
as a rule. I was surely glad the Walkers hadn't
had the sense to bring along some poison.
A dog's a dog, which means he's five-eighths stomach.

Thinking on this gave me bad ideas.
But I'll get to that when time is right. For now,
I called myself a lucky fool, out loud,
and bolted both dogs shut inside their houses

nights. I judged this thing would soon blow over.
I burned a yardlight too, which I'd never done.
And that (I guessed) was the last they'd come past dark.
You know, the funny part of this whole battle

up to now, when you consider who
I'd got myself involved with, was that neither
side had come right out into the open.
The only thing I knew for sure they'd done

was leave a mess of guts out on my lawn.
The only thing for sure they knew of me—
that I returned that mess to its right home.
The mailbox and the collar and the tracks....

For all we either knew, the Boss was making
visions in our eyes which, feeling righteous,
we took upon our *selves* to figure out.
And since, between the parties, I guessed *I*

had better claim to righteousness than they did,
I'm the one that—thinking back—began
to read the signs according to my will.
How many times have village hoodlums stove

a mailbox up? Or just plain village kids?
How many times, to mention what comes next,
has one old drunk shitkicker or another
raised some hell outside Ray Lawson's Auction

and Commission Sales on Friday night? And still,
I judged it was the Walkers who had slashed
all four of my new pickup's summer tires.
(Four months had passed.) And judged it quick as God.

The pickup spraddled like a hog on ice. It cost me
two hundred dollars just to run it home.
Next day I passed Short Jim as he came out
of Brandon's store and sized him up, and looked

at him: a man who'd killed another man,
but shyness in his eyes. He looked away.
And if *I'd* looked away just then.... Instead,
I saw a basket full of winter apples.

Baldwins mostly, full of slush and holes.
No wonder Brandon had that crop on sale!
Four cents each was asking more than enough
for winter apples still unsold in April.

If the top one hadn't had a hole as big,
almost, as half a dollar.... By God, where
would we be now? But there it was, the hole,
and I got notions. Maybe fate is notions

that you might have left alone, but took instead.
I did. I bought that apple, and another
just for show. And a box of pellets, too—
more rat pellets than I ever needed,

more than I could stuff into that hole
and still have stay enough in the rotten skin
to hold them in enough to fool a hog
that he *had* an apple. Walkers' hog, I mean.

They penned her on the far side of the road
from where that firetrap shack of theirs was built.
I didn't set right out. That apple sat
as much as seven days up on a post

of metal in the shed, where even rats
—Lord! let alone my kids—could never reach it.
And it sat inside my mind. Especially nights.
Or say it burned, the while I cooled myself

—or tried to do, with every nerve and muscle—
in bed, and said the same thing over and over:
"Nothing good will ever grow from feuds."
And just to get the apple *out* of mind,

spoke such damn foolishness you never heard:
"Old Mother Hubbard," "Stars and Stripes Forever"
(tried to get the words of one to go
along with the rhymes and rhythms of the other).

Then went down that seventh night, as if it was
another person who was going down
inside the shed (because the person I
believed I was kept up the sermon: "Nothing

any good from any feud," and so on),
picked the apple down, and put it in
my pocket, and—the moon was full—began
the uphill climb across the ridge. To Walkers'.

Stopped for breath at height of land, I turned
to see the house, where everyone was sleeping,
wondered what they dreamed, and if their dreams
were wild as mine become when moon's like that—

they say there's nothing in it, but as God
will witness me, a full moon fills my head,
asleep or not, with every bad idea.
One spring, the moon that big, a skunk came calling

in the shed, and my fool tomcat gave a rush.
The smell was worse than death. It woke me up,
if I was sleeping (I'd been trying to),
and till the dawn arrived, for hours I felt

the stink was like a judgment: every sin
from when I was a child till then flew back
and played itself again before my eyes.
High on the ridge, I felt I might reach out

and touch that moon, it was so close, but felt
that if I reached it, somehow it would burn.
It was a copper color, almost orange,
like a fire that's just beginning to take hold.

Your mind plays tricks. You live a certain while
and all the spooky stories that you read
or hear become a part of memory,
and you can't help it, grown or not, sometimes

the damnedest foolishness can haunt you. Owls,
for instance. I know owls. How many nights
do they take up outside, and I don't think
a thing about it? *That* night, though,

a pair began close by me. I'd have run,
the Devil take me, if the light had been
just one shade brighter, I'd have run right home
to get out of the woods or else to guard

the house, the wife, the kids. I don't know which.
A rat or mouse would shuffle in the leaves
and I would circle twenty yards around it.
I was close to lost until I found the brook

and waded it on down. It was half past two.
The moon kept working higher till I saw
the hog shed just across from Walkers' house.
There wasn't that much difference in the two.

I'm a man can't stand a mess. But they,
the boys and Sanitary Jim.... Well, they
can stand it. Seems that that's the way
that they *prefer* it. That hovel for the pig

was made of cardboard, chimney pipe, and wanes.
They'd driven I don't know how many sections
of ladder, side by side, into the mud
for fencing. Come the thaw each year, the ground

will heave that ladder up, and then you'll find
a pig in someone's parsnips. Anyway,
I looked the matter over, and the worry
that I'd felt about the thing that I was doing—

well, it went away. I felt as pure
as any saint or choirboy hunkered there.
I crept up on my knees and clapped the gate
(a box spring from a kid's bed) so the pig

would have a peek. I don't know why, exactly,
but I felt like watching as she took the apple
from my hand. It wouldn't do to leave it.
She just inhaled it, didn't even chew.

I backed up to the brook and watched some more,
then stepped in quick, because that poison sow
began to blow and hoot just like a bear.
The job was done. I hadn't left a track.

I don't know just what you'll make of this:
I fairly marched back up across the ridge
as if I made that climb four times a day.
The air was cold and sweet and clear, the way

it is when you can see the moon so plain.
I walked on to a beat and sang the hymns
—or sang them to myself—I'd got by heart
so many years before: "Old Rugged Cross"

and "Onward Christian Soldiers" and "Amazing
Grace," and never noticed how the cold
had numbed my feet till I was back in bed.
No one woke up. I slept two righteous hours.

You jump into a feud, and every trick's
like one more piece of kindling on the fire.
That's how I think of it, and you'll see why.
Come evening of the next day, I was sick.

You don't go paddling nighttimes in a brook
in April, and expect it's just a trick.
All night it felt like someone had a flatiron
and kept laying it between my shoulder blades.

My feet and legs were colored like old ashes.
My throat was sore enough I couldn't speak.
My wife, who didn't have a small idea
of where I'd been beside beneath the quilts,

lay it all to how I carried on.
"You've heard the old expression, 'sick with worry.'
That's what you've brought yourself, I think, from scheming
on those godforsaken Walkers." She was right,

but not the way she thought she was. In time,
there wasn't any use, I had to go
down to the clinic, twenty miles away.
You know those places: wait there half a day,

then let them pound you, scratch their heads, and scratch
some foolishness on a scrap of paper, wait
the other half while the druggist dubs around
to find the thing he's after. Come home poor.

If it was only poor that I came home!
I drove through town at fifteen miles an hour.
Swear to God I couldn't wheel it faster,
the way I was. It was a job to push

the throttle down, and I could scarcely see,
so blinked my eyes a time or two when I reached
the flat out by the pond. Above the ridge
the sky was copper-orange, and thick black smoke

was flying up to heaven, straight as string.
I thought I felt the heat. (But that was fever.)
By Jesus, that was *my* house. "Chimney fire,"
I said out loud, or loud as I could talk,

my throat ached so. The words were just a whisper,
and they sounded wrong the minute they came out.
I felt like I would die from all this sickness.
They called me "walking wounded" at the clinic:

pneumonia, but just barely, in one lung;
but now I felt my blood would burst the skin
and I'd just up and die inside that truck.
I squinched my eyes and lay the throttle on.

I meant to do some good before I died.
My wife was wrestling with a metal ladder
that had sat outside all winter, though I'd meant
to get it under cover every day.

I used it cleaning chimneys. It was stuck
in puddle ice beside the western wall.
I jumped out of the truck before it stopped,
and fell, and got back up, sweet Christ,

I tried to run, and every step I took
was like a step you take in dreams, the space
from road to house seemed fifteen thousand miles.
I stumbled to the shed and grabbed an ax

and put it to the ground to free the ladder,
but the ground just wouldn't give the damned thing up,
and every lick was like I swung the ax
from under water. I had no more force

than a kid or cripple. *My* kid, meanwhile cried
from behind a big storm window, "Daddy? Daddy?"
It sounded like a question. I gave up
and tried to call back up to him. I couldn't.

My words were nothing more than little squeaks,
and when they did come out, they were not plain.
And so my wife began to call the boy,
"Throw something through the window and jump out!"

He threw a model boat, a book, a drumstick.
He couldn't make a crack. I flung the ax.
It missed by half a mile. I threw again
and broke a hole, and scared the boy back in.

That was the last I saw him. Like a woman
sighing, that old house huffed once and fell.
Out back, beside the kennel, our baby daughter
danced and giggled to hear the howling dogs.

I went into a dead faint. And Hell could come
for all of me. And that is what has come.
Thirty years gone by since Lemmie Watson
broke my little mill of sticks and weeds

down by the brook, and I kicked the tar from him
and stayed indoors all week when school let out.
And Mrs. What's-Her-Name, I disremember,
fussing at her desk, would shake her head

and ask out loud if one small paddle wheel
was worth all this? I had to answer No.
I had to write it down, "No good can grow
from any feud." I wrote it fifty times

each afternoon. And then one afternoon
the Walker crew lay down a string of guts
across the road.... The part of life you think
you've got done living lies in wait like Satan.

For me, it was revenge. And what to do
right now? The house is gone, the boy, and I
believe I know just how they came to be.
But do I? Do I know what led to what

or who's to blame? This time I'll let it go.
No man can find revenge for a thing like this.
They say revenge is something for the Lord.
And let Him have it. Him, such as He is.

MANLEY

MANLEY

i.

It starts with a pair of pines, Manley high in air,
a boy even then obsessive. He grunted limb to limb,
sensing betrayal already. How could this tree be
the right one? "Simple," answered Reason, "The nest is here."

Oh yes. He'd observed the common crows for weeks at a time,
building from scroungings: chaff, paperscrap, weed, even bale-wire.
This morning at last he'd heard the froggy cries of the hatchlings.
Yet aloft, he felt something about that other pine...

It was much more fully needled and branched: he couldn't see
to trunk or crown, but there was something there, he thought,
as he looked up and across. Vaguely.

ii.

Something not reasonable, simple. One-handed, the going was hard,
the other fist gripping a feedbag gorged with batting.
He'd pluck the chick from the rank eyrie, sack it, fling it,
hope it landed softly. "A wild pet," he said

aloud, but dully, though the pine's string-thin top, near breaking,
careened with his weight and the wind. There was no rush or thrill:
below, the banal fields, dun, sun-bludgeoned cattle;
up here, the crows diving wildly at his head, strafing,

"like doubts," an older Manley might have said. His mind wandered;
he ignored the angry beaks, and that the bough might snap.
The other tree had turned suddenly darker....

iii.

That other, obscurer pine, its light or absence of light—
or not the tree nor the light, really, but a value he sensed
within: inclinations dawned that would ever haunt him.
He sought a prize. A presence. A not-quite-bodily weight.

An original something. The proverb concerning the "bird in the hand"—
he rejected it wholly, heaving out the burdenless burlap.
He wouldn't simply settle. He was bound to another dimension.
For years he would wonder, what, exactly, had prompted descent.

Had there been the weird metallic *scritch* the field guides describe?
No. A motion? No. Perhaps an aura? No.
The words he knew were too precise,

iv.

Like *glow, glimmer*: terms grafted on later, inane.
But something.... He wouldn't accept the notion of happenstance.
There was fate in that final turning, in what he perceived—a purpose.
Yet *did* he see the clownface, the shoulderless little frame?

Was there a sidewise scrabble of the saw-whet's claws, silly,
down a limb into viewless gloom? Or had it been a phantom
all this life? Manley thought so now and then,
as when he faced the faces of his students in Social Studies,

gray as untuned televisions. Blanks. Buzzes.
What he had to teach them he couldn't. Perhaps they were right:
Be dull, be happy. Stay to the surface.

v.

"The trouble is," the pupil began, urged by Manley
to disburden frankly the mind behind those smeary glasses
—"The trouble is, I just don't care what they were after,
Scott, Boone, Melville, Galileo, Curie ...."

At length the boy trailed off, hunching his mannish shoulders.
Semester's end: he'd heard these names since September, and others,
and strung them now in a wacky series. They were dead,
were the kind of torpid stuff that any teacher might conjure.

Manley could read the boy's thoughts (and wanted to thrash him)—
Dead matter from dead instructors: wasn't that their job?
So much for his *Motives of Exploration*....

vi.

Yet what on earth could be the motives of the *teacher*?
How explain they derived from an unseen bird in a pine?
When Manley's water-pump downcellar slipped its belt
and sounded *squee squee squee*, Manley, knowing better,

rushed out under the moon, hoping that he might see
—as once, perhaps, he saw—his bird, laughable, small.
Tell that to the boy, or anyone. Explain the passage
on an old Gene Ammons album of "Willow, Weep for Me,"

when Gene clamps the reed into demi-quavers recalling
... what? What he thought, hearing, to see, or the other way round?
While the crows were attacking, the darkness falling.

vii.

"And if I say, 'Surely the darkness will cover me,
and the light around me turn to night,' darkness is not
dark to you; the night is as bright as the day...." "Says who?"
breathed Manley. Said the parson, reading the Psalm by Manley's

friend Jim's coffin. July. Sweat. And next,
Amos's shaggy-dog questions: "Do two walk together, unless
they have made an appointment?... Does a bird fall in a snare on earth"
—Manley straightened—"when there is no trap for it?" Perplexed,

guilty as ever, Manley considered his life all wrong:
he should have been thinking of Jim; but the blocks' and ropes' squealing
put him in mind of the saw-whet's "song."

viii.

Was he ever satisfied, completely? Everything happened,
so it seemed to him, at once. Of course there was snow,
and sun and rain, and fog especially, and calendars changed;
and yet the days from the pine to now were a single season,

in which, wild-birdlike himself, he fluttered out into weather
at the passing of a round, small shadow across his mind,
or across a window, or at the scraping sound of cello,
tire, cat, whatever. And did he alter, you wonder,

when at last they confronted each other in a shower of Perseids?
How might I know myself? I cannot say, not really.
To see it, his life gathered—or I must imagine it did:

finally to see it. Small, elusive, ludicrous, holy.

www.ingramcontent.com/pod-product-compliance
Lightning Source LLC
LaVergne TN
LVHW041536060526
838200LV00037B/1011